WHY SPEAK?

ALSO BY NATHANIEL BELLOWS

On This Day: A Novel

WHY SPEAK?

Poems

NATHANIEL BELLOWS

W. W. NORTON & COMPANY

NEW YORK LONDON

For information about permission to reproduce selections from this book, write to Permissions,
W. W. Norton & Company, Inc., 500 Fifth Avenue, New York, NY 10110

Manufacturing by Courier Westford
Book design by Chris Welch
Production manager: Julia Druskin

Library of Congress Cataloging-in-Publication Data

Bellows, Nathaniel.
Why speak? : poems / Nathaniel Bellows. —1st ed.
p. cm.
ISBN-13: 978-0-393-06240-3
ISBN-10: 0-393-06240-6
I. Title.
PS3602.E65W48 2007
811'.6–dc22

W. W. Norton & Company, Inc., 500 Fifth Avenue, New York, N.Y. 10110
www.wwnorton.com

W. W. Norton & Company Ltd., Castle House, 75/76 Wells Street, London W1T 3QT

1 2 3 4 5 6 7 8 9 0

For my family

Contents

ONE

FOUR

Acknowledgments

Grand Street: "Alfalfa Farm"; *The Massachussetts Reveiw:* "Five Funerals," "Why Speak?"; *The New England Review:* "Ornithology," "Russian Birch"; *The New Republic:* "Open Letter Re: The Good Fight," "Elegy"; *The New York Times Book Review:* "Harm's Woods"; *Open City:* "A Certain Dirge," "An Attempt," "At the House on the Lake"; *The Paris Review:* "Removal," "Some Traditions," "At the Symphony," "Liberty Island"; *Ploughshares:* "Myopia"; *Prairie Schooner:* "Every Hour Here," "Quarry"; *Southwest Review:* "Plum Island"; *TriQuarterly:* "The Good Shepherd"; *Western Humanities Review:* "Music Lessons," "Vocations"; *Witness:* "Foaling"; *The Yale Review:* "Work."

"Liberty Island" appeared in the anthology *Poems of New York,* published by Everyman Publishers, September 2002.

A very special thank-you to Richard Howard.

Thank you: Jill Bialosky, Evan Carver, Lucie Brock-Broido, Elizabeth Schmidt, Melanie Rehak, and David McCormick.

Thank you: ARB, JFB, MBB, KRB, RVVW, RGS, and all my friends for their love and support.

ONE

ALFALFA FARM

From the highway I see the open, unmown fields, two silos the same
battered blue, the sign with its white letters still singing the name

ALFALFA FARM. And next door, the house of an old friend, long gone,
now redone and different from how I knew it: raw, dug-up lawn,

cracked storm door, a van in the driveway balanced on blocks where
his sisters would play under a pile of ratty afghans. We watched them

from an appliance box with a slot cut out for spying. Now there is
a birdbath, a potting shed where their mildewed dollhouse sagged.

The farm is unchanged. Barns upon barns, the same cows wearing
the same canvas hoods alongside the highway where the cars fly by.

We used to count them: cows and cars, out in the field for no other reason
than to stay out of his house where Christmas lights, cheap cordials,

Easter grass lay around for no discernable holiday, the same warped box
of a chocolate sampler spoiling on the counter. For the flies, I thought.

The flies that clung to the eyes of beasts in the barns, ate their fill
from around the lids, flew up in a frenzy when we ran through the kitchen.

The same flies, calves, and shabby stallions in the fields. I see them all
as I pass by on the highway. The falling sign, crooked like a sleeping head,

the rusted tractor punctured by reeds in the swamp. This new house
has a gazebo in the yard where we stood on the stone wall, watched

men slaughter the black bulls they'd linked to a concrete slab by the rings
in their snouts. The air was sharp with blood and howls and struggle,

the men took running starts, gouged the bulls with pikes, dragged them
down the hill where they bled a dark blot of blood on the pond.

This is not the same house—now it's painted sky blue with white trim, crisp
as an unsliced cake beneath a plastic dome—not the same house I

barely remember leaving. My friend's sisters wore their bathing suits
all day, his mother was locked in the bathroom with a stranger whose car

was parked on the lawn. The manure cooked, piled in its rank monument.
I was a child then. I believe that was a part of my childhood.

RUSSIAN BIRCH

Is it agony that has bleached them to such beauty? Their stand
is at the edge of our property—white spires like fingers, through which
the deer emerge with all the tentative grace of memory. Your father

loved these trees. When you try to imagine his childhood, it is all old
footage, in a similar scheme: black and white. But he died, and all you know
is that they reminded him of home. As they remind you he is gone

to a country as unimaginable as his life before you were born, before
the woman who would be your mother lived as she does now—lost,
wandering at the edge of her life's whitened gates.

After a storm, one birch fell in the field, an ivory buttress collapsed across
the pasture. Up close there is pink skin beneath the paper, green lichen
ascending in settlements of scales. In the dark yard it beckons you back

to snow, the static of the past—your father, a boy, speaking in a tongue
you never knew, calling down from the branches. Or the letter you wrote
to a mother you weren't allowed to miss—black ink scrawled across

the white pulp of the page: *I am very lonely without you.*

THE GOOD SHEPHERD

Saved from the slaughter, our new ewe yanked my mother
down the street; I saw their struggle on the sidewalk.

It was fall and the fair shrieked beyond the field.
I parked cars in our back pasture, bills wadded thick in my pocket.

I handled money all morning, made change, overcharged, flagged
drivers away from where the marsh trespassed into the field.

I spent hours pushing stuck cars, passengers stood aside clutching
over-sized stuffed animals like starched children, garishly dyed.

All night the ewe bleated from its stall under the barn;
we heard it at dinner, during dishes, lying in our beds

blending with the distant voice of the square-dance caller,
the metallic trill of the calliope, the heavy exhale of the rides

ascending into the sky, packed with passengers whose remote
screams mimicked the last mosquitoes of the season, still alive

in our rooms. This would be the first of many sheep
my mother stored under the barn. No one could say a thing.

How many times had we watched the parade pass before our house
each shabby float barely balanced on an old station wagon, Girl Scouts

flinging salt-water taffies, the marching band blaring *Oh When the Saints*,
pausing, to shake the spit from their horns?

Every fall we stood on the sidewalk, my mother's hand outstretched
as the sheep rolled by in their tractor-pulled pens. Always had me hold

her coat as she ran alongside, her hand buried in the oily wool, resting
on each head as my hand would rest on the cool chrome of her car each

time she drove out the driveway. I would chase her. It was a game,
a practicing, as the car slid out from under my hand the way coins slide

hesitantly from one palm to the other, or into the mouth of a jar, or
as the dart's departure from the well-intentioned grip takes its leave

as the fair does, suddenly, without fair warning, each lynchpin pulled,
flatbeds packed, hauling onto the highway.

REMOVAL

They carried the lamps out as if they were children.
Rugs were laid out on the grass, or beaten
with a shovel on the clothesline.

Boxes were labeled in scrawl, stacked in the yard
like stout chimneys. Where were you
when "Kitchen" split down the center

and silver spun down the stairs, a pear knife
lost for an hour in a coil of the hose? Did you
see them haul out the clock, wrapped in blankets, a sick man

carried to his car? Or pieces of the piano
in procession, strings whining,
pulling at their pins in the evening air?

As night seeped under the eaves, they broke apart
the upstairs windows. In the half light it was lowered:
the fat white bathtub dangling like a weighing calf.

We all cheered as it floated above us, cupping our hands
as the tiny feet came to rest in our palms. Through the hole
we could see into the bathroom. Your arms were like those curtains,

drifting now as you dragged on your cigarettes,
tilting to breathe the cool air, your lungs clotted
like a closet full of coats; the ones we hid in on each visit,

those we had emptied that day, packing
the darkness we once disappeared into. Where were you
as we huddled there, gripping the porcelain knob?

They carried us out to the lawn, the grass
cold in the shade of the trees: we are standing now where
they take up the water pipe that runs down to the lake;

where we swam as children, paddling
as the water slowly drained around us, siphoned up the hill,
filling your salted bath where you lay for hours, steeping.

A CERTAIN DIRGE

The metronome tocked like the bird that beats
its head against the trees in the yard;

our piano's room faced the street my sister crossed
to the neighbor's house where horses gnawed the lawn, where

the echo of the car's screaming brakes was our dog's howl—
it had followed her across and was hit, I heard it because

I was practicing, pedaling, hands separately, each piece
repeated over the sound of our dog, of my sister, inconsolable,

beating the bushes outside the window where our dog
would die and be buried that night in the rain.

I heard the car strike the dog over the sound
of each felt-covered mallet striking taut wound wires.

I did not stop, even when my sister's barrette bobbed
at the window, even when she begged me to help her find

the dog hiding under the house, scratching
against the concrete foundation—the sound

of stones collected on the beach
clattering upstairs in the dryer.

PARTS OF SPEECH

Because I chewed consonants like cud,
J and G, S slurring over my tongue,
the intercom barked my name, summoned me
to meet with Mrs. Weston, our speech teacher—
her office in the basement of the school.

Walking home I would struggle to recite as if still
speaking to the tape. On the tractor, mowing the fields
I hissed my exercises, enunciating the names
of fruit trees, spinning the blades close
to their slender, wrapped trunks.

In bed I spoke into the folded face of my pillow,
remembering the dull sound of her clogs
slipping off onto the rug under the table, the vowels that heaved
inside her sweater rising over my bed as a singer's held note;
I slept to that sound, woke to it ringing

as the high feedback pitch of the intercom, calling me
from my class down each week to the room
next to the furnace where she sat silent, her hand
lost in her hive of hair,
recovering comb after comb.

I spoke and spat, she chewed on the frayed tip
of an eraser, watching my mouth. Sometimes
she held my jaw in her hand, delicately, as if with
inspection, as one might hold a piece of fruit, considering.

AT THE HOUSE ON THE LAKE

My uncle said: you're prettier
than your sister, let himself hang
out of his shorts and took my hand.
We were looking for the salt lick, deer bait, twine,
searching the boathouse by the breakwater.

Outside my brother and sister swam, dived
for coins they'd found in the seats of the car.
The canoe, leashed by the prow to the pier,
echoed to its own empty sound, swung
wide, like an opening door, out into the lake.

We ate our meals under startled deer twisting
from the walls, painted fish mounted on plaques.
Our aunts served, circled the table wearing oven
mitts, aprons smeared with what steamed before us
in chipped porcelain bowls.

Prayers before bed, my hands made the shape
of a sail or the wedge our uncles used to split
wood in the yard—fallen limbs, yanked stumps, sturdy
trees that once hung the trapped hare, nailed through its paws
to the trunk. My brother and sister dared me to touch its silver

fur, unbloodied beneath the chin. But I could not; each night
while the house slept, I stood on the couch to touch
the deer's glass eye, set like a jewel in its stiff socket—
the chiseled stones our aunts wore, antique rings
my sister would inherit—like those jewels,

only more beautiful.

HORTICULTURAL

I could not saw the fallen tree—not all
of it had fallen—because somehow each spring,
the rotted half still mysteriously bloomed.

In the orchard we hung iron fruit, syrup-coated
decoys to fool devouring convoys of insects.
The harvest suffered but survived the early frost,
and we grew sick of the sweetness of peaches.

We ate from the garden till it was spent, then
threw its left-behinds at each other—failures
still in their beds, scabbed over with saltmarsh hay.

Although the holly never went out of leaf,
we only clipped the branches, the berries
for the cold season when Joy took root in the house
and crept from room to room like a scarlet vine.

IN GREATER DETAIL

I cannot help thinking of you in your panicked state, cleaning
in the early morning, waking me from the sleep you're deprived of—

I am halfway up the stairs to my appointment when I hear a vacuum
howling three floors above me. Someone is whistling, it echoes in the hall

of the brownstone. Beneath my boots, white scraps of paper glow
luminous against the deep red of the stair carpet. I cannot help thinking

of my birthday geese—their feathers were whitest against the wet
carmine of their insides: one torn apart by the dog, the other,

asleep in a thicket, crushed by the bulldozer hired to level the garden.
The geese were a gift. They caught me off guard the day

I received them: a lunging ambush, a fury of dirty ivory, red eyes, red
webbed feet flung from the boughs of the ash, screeching as they beat

my face with their velvet heads. The paper on the stairs must have fallen
from a hole in a box—the box holding something fragile, the paper packed

to protect the gift inside. Someone left this trail to the door behind which
the doctor sits in his dimly lit room where I open my mouth and remove

memory like a pit pried from a fruit, a prize pulled from a holiday
cake. You served me my cake with its eight lit candles—frosted white as

the geese, as the paper—the cake lopsided, slightly burned, as cakes baked
in old ovens often are. At the end of the hour I leave; the stairs

are clean. A swift hand high above me waxes the wooden banister
with a rag. Behind the wall the doctor's muffled voice begins speaking

to a patient who has come in through a different door. I cannot help thinking
of you, coming in my room in the morning, pulling up rugs to beat

on the line outside. You never meant to wake me. I always pretended to be
asleep while you worked around my bed in the dark. In the brownstone

the stair carpet is gouged—red and spotless, and on this day
someone here has received a gift—a box filled with paper and glass.

SOME TRADITIONS

Like the bogs that pulled the warriors down,
weighed by armor and regalia,
stewing and steeping, tender

skinned fruit hardening
in the sun—only in darkness;
we were celebrated.

We were ruined.

The men came, scraped and painted the front of the house,
leaving the sides to peel. First it was the chairs
that grew tiny tags like leaves,

then others were sold. The drawers
were full of unpaid bills, tied with ribbon like cakes;
coins of wax in dotted lines up the stairs.

The radiators stood in an awkward swirl.

No more days of crinoline or hedges shaped
like fish and bears. The curtains came down and were
shredded, twisted, stuffed under doors.

The piano remained in the hall, like an obelisk,
as if to haunt the place we had to leave;
it would have played on its own, we knew,

had we not robbed it of its keys.

FIVE FUNERALS

One with five caskets heaved from the hearse
rolling past me in the pew.

Five new blazers bought, one sewn with a secret
pocket for my coins—hidden from the passed

basket of bills. Different light, all the same stories
in the windows. One church, one stench, one sermon,

five: shake your neighbor's hand. One hole, five
stones, one name carved in script.

Five wakes stocked with flowers arranged in rings,
one open casket, five grave family faces, one

book to be signed; five signatures, improving. Five
guilty rides on the limousine's blue plush seats. One

magnetic flag stuck to the hood leading us through red
lights of five different towns. Five of us in the back,

one of us waving. I was waving to people watching
on the street, drivers waving us through.

One funeral. I had not yet turned eleven.
One One the cake would say that summer.

Five caskets, one organ droning, five
hundred hymns in the book, opened to one that made

everybody cry. No one could sing or say the words.
The priest offered us the wafer—I was afraid

of its taste. Five robed boys carried candles behind
the caskets. We followed the hearse. Five rectangular holes

surrounded by plastic grass. We will all be one, says the priest,
with our maker. They could not make me

take the wafer. All before I was eleven. Still ten—five years past
five years old when the funeral began. One day I put on

a suit, the church was cold, I sang with the organ. Then began
the caskets. One just like the next.

TWO

ELEGY

An egret lifting its blue feet in the reeds, among the cut-up
sticks floating in the shallows of the lake. What caught my eye
was its color—beyond white, white moving past itself
into something lit, as if with winter's last light. The water was gray—
I should say that the water was black, because, against it,
the bird glowed, plumage like an over-powdered pastry.
There were flowers, too. And green buds on the trees, like flecks
of food scattered on a sleeve. Otherwise, there was little
hue to report. You should have seen that bird—not its coat
but the way it moved reminded me of the blind, how they
pause before they walk, calibrating their movements
like a clock. Once, when my watch had stopped, I opened its face
and peered at its frozen parts and felt as I did
peering through the reeds at the bird: disbelief combined
with fatigue: the list of misunderstood things extends: the bird,
the watch, the blind . . . where are you among them? The bird plodded
through some floating trash, at which point I left not to
have to see it struggle with the bright wrappers. I don't know
what happened after that—where the bird stepped, or, if its beak
pierced the black lake, or if, when it flew away, it was absorbed by the sky . . .
I wondered what you'd say about all this. Maybe you'd suggest
it was the crocuses, actually, hundreds of pale shells, each
with a tiny votive flame that gave the day its brightness.

PANGAEA

Halfway home my car window snaps and falls into the slot
of the door. I drive in gloves and hat, feathers of ice frame
the windshield until there is just a bull's-eye of road—a ship's
porthole, the aperture of the sugared Easter egg, with its simple
pastel scene inside, smuggled in our pockets, secretly licked

as we sang in the bright church—the same church where I
staggered with my brother up the stone steps, under the casket
of an uncle who had smoked out every badger in the yard,
nailed each to a tree by its paws. . . . At the wake, everyone smirked
as we set pillows on the floor, did headstands against the walls—

our loafers and party shoes skidding tiny arcs on the wallpaper.
Afterward, we emptied out candy dishes, left wrappers on the table
uncurling slowly from their wads—gold, like the sparks the farrier
flung, beating shoes into shape each spring. I woke those mornings
to her hammering echoing off the barn walls, marking the lambs'

clumsy steps, awkward as marionettes—one lamb soon to be torn
apart by the dog and hauled in a grain bag to a trench in the orchard
where we circled the site and sobbed. . . . At night, we stood on apple
crates to braid the horse's mane, twisted each tress with elastics.
His iron shoes chipped the cement floor and would soon stamp

a perfect crescent into the car door—bucking, crazed, his eyes dark
and wet as the syrup that drips from the silver taps of every
driveway maple in our town. Our town—asleep, silent as I drive
through, caught behind plows grinding at the roads, spitting out
salt. The storm is done, cars and homes rounded-over like loaves.

I turn and drive along the river, a black smear of moving water cuffed
by ice. My headlights pick up strange eyes darting from the woods,
glowing like polished coins, an opened locket, the camping lantern
twinned against the amber water where we waded in the summer,
found shards of china painted with flowers, a rusted gun barrel,

hundreds of fireflies pressed into the bank, stitched like the stars
we named as we lay in our beds, quilts and sheets wrapped around us
as the waves would on our beach, where we'd stand peering beyond
the islands at that other rind of land above the horizon—thin and fine
as the layer peeled from our bodies when the sun torments our skin.

HARM'S WOODS

On the way to Harm's Woods
did you haul the basket? Your brothers
spiraling, arms-outstretched airplanes
bombing acorns at splintered picnic

tables scrawled with names, stained red
from your parents' spilled wine, cork thrown
in the stream, floating as a boat for
the boys, bottle submerged, trapping

the tadpole fluttering up the dark green neck.
Your mother sets it, retrieved, in the center,
her blue teeth biting a slice of pear, your father
spying on sunbathers, pretending to read.

The wagging ferns, agreeing together
in the breeze, hide your feet, your knees.
You unwrap the wax-paper lunch slowly,
the way someone might undress a doll. . . .

In Harm's Woods, did you stumble, lopsided
with the basket? Every Sunday after church,
new car, best clothes, families stationed
on the grass, high-flying kites staked down.

FOALING

The hay was wet with blood and something that looked like tea.
In the boughs of the firs behind the barn, where the chickens roost
and drop their waste on the rusted car's hood, the cock was crowing.
He cries at all hours for no reason. One time he cried all night

and no one came. The next day half the hens were gone—only feathers left
in wads around the yard. With thick cotton swabs the stablehand cleaned
the mare's opening—it had been torn, stuck with hay from the stall's
floor. Everyone winced when they wiped her down. A stablehand put

the mare's head between his knees to steady her. She was making low
noises while the colt stood beside her, tottering like a flimsy chair.
I know the mare because she kicked a hole in my car door. My neighbors
woke me up, called me early to come and help with the birth.

The mare was on its side, heaving into the straw. A stablehand had his
hands inside the mare. He pulled out two legs and worked them like
the handles of a bellows or a hedge clipper, trying to get the colt out.
I stood against the stall door beside the hanging bridles and girths.

Somewhere in the trees, the cock was crowing. It keeps the neighborhood
awake. A fox had slaughtered the chickens. I live across the street
and found feathers clogged like foam in the front hedges. A fox had stolen
one of my geese from the pen. I saw it in the orchard eating the white bag.

I knew the mare because once she jumped a rail and ran into my yard.
I found her in the orchard, rearing up to strip the fruit from the highest
branches. She would not let me get close enough to grab her halter.
She would not let the stablehands pull the colt out, the two legs dangled

from between her legs. The blanket by her head was soaked with blood
because the bit had broken in her mouth. By now the heat of morning
had set in, and everyone was sweating. Dust from the hay and swarms
of flies clogged the air. Behind the barn the cock kept crowing. The cock

will be killed because of all the complaints. The couple next door says it
wakes their newborn. It was not supposed to live: the child born early
and with a bad heart. I saw the family pushing a stroller. It seemed to take no
effort. The child was inside, wrapped in a blanket and small as a thermos.

When the colt finally emerged it lay unhinged next to a sack that looked
like liver. The stablehands threw the sack to the dogs to fight over.
The mare lay back and ignored the colt, which tried to stand but unfolded
like a fallen tent. A stablehand turned on the hose and filled buckets

with water. He added iodine and salt, staining his hands as he mixed.
With a knife I shaved soap into a bucket to wash down the horses.
The shavings were white like the feathers I'd found in the fields—the place
the fox had gone to finish the goose. In a shaded spot beneath the trees.

PLUM ISLAND

Not really an island. It is connected to mainland by marsh,
bogs that from the low-slung drawbridge look like ant
tunnels, those sandwiched between panes and called farms.

A colony of shacks, trailers, beachcombers, bathers,
those that come to fish or spy on the endangered
in the Sanctuary, which it isn't when trucks plow

through dunes, partygoers scorch the sand,
dousing seagulls with lighter fluid to laugh at the bird,
which flies in flames, crying its same stupid cry.

And the ocean warms with death; three local fishermen
lost in their whaler during the storm, missing for days
while the water drummed its fists against the shore.

The drunks at the SandBar half listen, tilt stools forward
toward the news. Under umbrellas, couples fool around
on beach chairs with a strange new thrill, charged

by the stench that fringes the air, sharper than exhaust,
the smell of the kill coming fresh off the sea.
The bodies wash up dyed blue as eggs, the rings

around their salted eyes, the moons beneath their nails
wear the deep bruise of sweet pitted fruit, the crop that
once flourished here, plentiful, spoiling on the boughs.

QUARRY

Everyone swims where a car careened down the wall of rock,
six silent passengers, crammed like clowns that night,
moths swarming headlights, bright sinking moons white

as your shoulders below me, beckoning me over the edge.
Behind you three teenagers balance on the slimy log
—an old telephone pole—running as it spins, falling

face first into the green. You swim side-stroke
as you were taught: *pick an apple, put it in the basket*,
whirling around like an otter, your bright bank of teeth

flashing back at me. My piano teacher who lived nearby
said the granite crew, with all their equipment, drowned
when they hit a spring; the hole filled like a bath,

and with the water rose lunch boxes, helmets, newspapers,
skimmed by a rowboat, slicing the quarry's new skin.
Flags flew half-mast in front of the unfinished library.

When I jump, I fear the smack as I hit, drilling down
into depths you assure me are miles below where we kick
our legs. Over there, near the lower ledges, a dog dives,

retrieves a mottled buoy in its mouth, children run on
slanted rocks, inflatable wings slipping down their arms,
the lid of a Styrofoam cooler flips off, lands on the water

where, like a speckled iceberg, it floats away. You shriek,
peering down at dark eels passing between us, scraping against
our calves, cold thick cables come up from their caves.

SELDOM SEEN

I spend all morning looking at a book of rooms—photographs of rooms
in houses where no one lives. A kitchen stove is covered with duck-green tiles,
on a landing, a stout clock conceals a music box, in a child's bedroom

a painting of a bulb-shaped whale. The book's text explains the painting's
value—the image's "seldom-seen" quality. The artist had obviously never seen
a whale, since it resembled nothing like what I once saw—not a

shapeless ship-tipper, but a tapered, heaving beast, its tail like a blade.
Our captain alerted us to crowd the starboard railing and the pitch-colored
thing surfaced, its skin grooved and wet like a snow tire. It turned away

from us as a sleeping person will when a curtain parts, or how a bather
starts when intruded upon . . . this morning, I woke thinking: where are you
now? Am I too late to see you again? I am. I will always be.

The whale was not aware of our eyes on its markings—a painter's tarp
or a hand-painted wrap as if someone's hand had painstakingly applied
each spot and streak of gray and white. Like in these rooms where alcoves

are painted with gardens, thick bowers where birds preen in the leaves, a
fountain spouts beside a hedge of topiary deer. I've seen deer near every
house I've ever lived in. Once, I saw a pair standing in the tide pools;

I saw one eating flowers on the median by the shopping center; and one
in pieces on the road—the way you must have looked, struck down just
yesterday. All the deer were dull brown. And you, my friend, are long

gone. Above where a child slept the whale devours a dory. A man at
the helm gouges its eye with a harpoon. The moon is wide and high, lanterns
spray spikes of light. I see how the artist made it all up—I know the need,

the penchant for invention. In the museum at the whale boat launch,
there were similar paintings, and harpoons on the walls above mason jars of
cloudy golden oil. Soon we would see the whale lolling in the green,

spouting from its hole, which is concealed until its breath escapes. As yours
did—as you did, having disappeared to some unknown place . . . to this house,
perhaps, invisible, unadorned, where every room is an empty ornament.

MARKED

With the nervous precision of a guest
toweling a glass in a house
where every dish is hand-dried,

I conjure up the scarf of poison
ivy on your neck, spread to mine.
We ached in the itch

in separate rooms, mouths marked
from sharing the same cup, same spoon, all
we touched boiled now for others to use.

Years since that poor hotel—the landing adorned
with its false *Primavera* as we ran upstairs.
Our room was like the hallway only

behind a door. The bed was large, on wheels
yet bolted to the wall.
We shared a bathroom with other guests,

answered their questions and wore the slant grins
of the newly, yet not-nearly wed.
With the brazen insolence of the unwelcome,

we soaked the room with smell and sound,
left it ravaged, in retrospect, ruined as
we would be . . . and being so, branded.

MYOPIA

Yes, they were like windows, all those medical jars,
not the eyes themselves. No, they were like acorns,
or rocks, hard, solid things—enemies of glass—yet
kept safe, sealed, untouched, behind glass.

Every day I would scrutinize the jars, take them
one by one from their organized comb in the bottom
bureau drawer of my father's study. I spent hours
on the floor of that dusty room examining the vials,

each containing an eye—saved from his research
in foreign countries—left lonely, unpaired, a broken
chunk of cork trapped at the base of a bottle:
Horse, Monkey, Human, Hare. . . .

Some were hard skinned with a rugged layer of crust,
some floated, spun, sank in speckled bog water,
others were, as if by a mistake, perfect, the way
I pictured an eye to be—except in a jar—lolling

backward, forward as I tilted the glass in the C-clamp
of my fingers, watching it roll from end to end,
imagining a tonsil in the soprano's throat, rolling with
her voice rolling on the radio downstairs in the kitchen;

where my mother sang, too, balling melon for a party.
I heard them through the vents—invisible tunnels sewn into

the house; we hear each other, everywhere—could they hear
the subtle scrape, my lashes against the glass?

The thin wall separating me from a *Mink's* gauzy eye?
Perhaps the same *Mink* hanging skinned, one of how many
in the hall closet? Worn one winter night as we
stood on the walk, gawking at the accident:

black ice, sirens, a man crushed into the steering wheel,
the plush column of my mother herding us indoors. . . .
Downstairs, that soprano soaring, her voice jumping up
the register, I'd shake the glazed orb of *Goat*; it played

like a rubber ball thudding against the glass.
With the held high note fluttering over the blender,
I removed *Infant*, whose eye was small, caked, fused
with its own rough skin to the side of the jar. Even when

turned upside-down it stuck, immobile as a chrysalis:
those we gathered for school, feeling shame. No, not shame,
some reluctance, though, when the worm slid from its silver-
minted pod. We saw the rusted wings extend, watched

it's first flight like a poorly made paper plane that soars,
unfolds. *Infant* eye, never used, No, perhaps used a day or two,
in what place? Hospital, taxicab, rented room with
a corner sink, blue-stained smear beneath the faucet. . . .

I removed them all, a Stonehenge on the sun-drenched carpet.
Bowling pins, chess figures, I lay eye-level with them, focused
as the sunlight worked its way through whatever translucence
was left glossy, without patina, tunneled inside each eyeball.

Now I shut off the lights in the apartment, lie on my bed
in the streetlamp-streaked dark, scrutinizing the grid
of lit windows across the street: amorous couple overlapping
on a red couch, father strutting in his underwear, woman

hauling out her harp on Sundays an hour before
the quartet arrives, prying open their velvet-lined cases.
More interesting than violin lessons shrieking in my building,
thunder of the trash chute, snoring couple next door. . . .

These people in their lighted cells across the street must
see me here, typing, making my bed, must have watched
me risk life and limb, leaning out to clean the glass
coated thick with grime that reveals itself in streaks when

the sun comes in to fade my blankets, bleach jackets of books,
kill the jade plant my father gave me when I moved in. Yes,
too much light—not my erratic watering, not my lack of pruning.
No, my mistake; I set it in that place to watch it grow.

THREE

FIVE PAINTINGS BY HOWARD PYLE

"So the treasure was divided" 1905

As it always is when there is a death. Or a heist or a highjacking
of a galleon—chests split open, bouillon weighed, bitten, divided.
The pirates adorn themselves as they count, *sing their dearest songs*
as the sun lays its golden tongue across the waves.

You drove in with the pickup filled, everything covered in blankets,
wrapped, battened down with plastic cord. We unloaded it all, went
to work reassembling your sudden inheritance: two beds, a bureau,
and the massive hutch, looming like a bower in the kitchen: every

drawer, every door had a knob adorned with a painted bird—America's
bald eagle perched on a dense nest of flags and arrows. Each more
frightened than the next. Beaks screaming for release. The flock totaled
twenty or more. (So many birds trapped in tiny glass knobs!)

You plan to replace them so we unscrewed each one, stored them
in the laundry room where your Aunt resides, sealed in a box, heavy
as a charred loaf. The pirate's fire burns on the beach. *And the brightest
things that are theirs* they sleep with, stow away inside their clothes.

They sit in a circle, sorting, hoarding the ship's scattered bounty.
While for weeks you wake each morning with a sense of loss. Searching
each room as if there had been a theft. No. Just the opposite.
Her house inside your house.

"She drew her bridle, listening—there was no sound" *1905*

The backfire of the septic truck rang like a cannon. What I imagined
the cannon, frozen and plugged on the Common, would sound like.
Where bronze soldiers stood silently, hefting a flag into the air;
a plaque, as in a museum, bore the artist's name, date of the cast.

A gun someone was firing in their yard? It was the septic truck
and it's driver, Charlie Linehan, leaking waste like a leash.
I would see Charlie at the roller rink, leering at middle-aged mothers
in threadbare leotards doing stretches on mats, the stereo blaring.

The woman in this painting is young. She has dark hair and holds a gun.
She is on her horse in the forest, at a halt. Whereas my sister was riding
hers along the road, the septic truck following behind her.
The firing gun was the exhaust pipe because the truck was idling low.

The dark-haired woman is shown in a wooded place where the light
is sparse. *She drew her bridle.* She has a small silver pistol in her hand. *She
drew* a pistol. The painter *drew* the pistol in her hand, she and her horse
alone in a darkening wood. My sister's braid hung under

her helmet, a bell's rope, the helmet because the horse had once
thrown her off. The horse gets spooked easily—a loud noise, thunder
that sends the dogs under our beds. I saw Charlie Linehan in his truck
trailing my sister. She would not look behind her. I was on my bike

44

behind them. The woman's eyes are frightened, she has a hood over
her head. They have that in common, their heads are hidden. My sister's
helmet, covered in green and gold silk, glowed in the dense autumn light.
Wherever the horse set down its feet, their shadow bled across the road,

the soldiers' shadow bled down the side of their monument the way
a sundial's rod casts its shadow across the numbered plate—remarkably
accurate, this clock; no gears, *no sound*. The sculpture's shadow moves
across the Common, over the grass under which they all lay buried.

The young woman raises her head, *listening*. The gun fired, rang across
the field where my sister rode for hours. More rust than red, that truck.
The bronze soldiers, green over the years. Beneath their helmets their faces
are drawn, tired from their days of protecting our town.

"Then the real fight began" 1908

Where it always begins. With every sleepless night. Every morning
when the brightly lit, perfectly crisp autumn day is the only reason
to stay indoors. Behind doors. With every mirror draped in a sheet
to keep shame at bay. In the tradition of some family's funeral,
the mirror's eye, lidded like a drawn blind.

This is the mutiny the body pits against itself. The rebellion
of the crew against their captain. The hoard of sailors approaching
the porthole, where their leader (seen here as just a hand holding
a smoking gun) has stowed himself below deck. There is no safe place
on this or any ship. No distant slice of land or bird to promise land.

The painting depicts the moment after the captain fires when
the real fight begins. The sun-bleached deck, the red bandanna tied
around a sailor's scalp, the brushed blue of the ocean, these are choices
the artist made because . . . of the beauty inherent in upheaval? Am I right?
The captain will pay for his mistreatment of those who once admired him.

I will pay for my own mistreatment. My missing admiration. This mutiny,
like the rallies in the newspaper: Choose Life! Somewhere in the world
the real fight begins and I am especially drawn to these stories. Someone
wrote it all down. Someone snapped the shot of the child . . . dead? asleep?
in an oil drum. Loud voices all night from the street. I hear them fighting

below my window. Let them fight. Let me know who is fighting and how they fare. Let me alone and I promise to bother no one. Promise apology to those I have misled. Those who feel I have misled them. A captain is always outnumbered, but the worst is their betrayal: they loved him, followed him to sea. And now they want no part in it.

"Her head and shoulders hung over the space without" **1904**

The dancer died during her performance. She died unexpectedly
while she was performing. She remembers thinking: I have died.

She remembers hearing the music, the fall of the other dancer's feet who
left her body untrodden, as if in their weeks of practice, learned

she would die for those brief moments and rise in perfect time
to join them, see the dance to its end.

A couple is arguing at a window. The woman leans out over the ledge.
Her body, a shadowed vine or a curtain seeking *the space* outside

the opened sash. The man keeps her inside with both his hands.
His face is angry, pained with fear and love. The paint is heavily

applied, perhaps with a palette knife, cold dark hues that denote
the hours before morning.

After three years apart we meet by chance. She tells me over dinner
that she died during her performance. How she cried after the audience

left, because, in her words, she did not mind. Surprised herself
with her own resolve. She spoke with a pained expression. But

without fear. Her hands rose before her, drawing her words forward
like a conductor who draws forth an orchestra's measured sound—

her hands assembling something in the air, hands that once had sought my
skin beneath my cuff and collar . . . *Ah! Then, if mine had been*

the Painter's hand, To express what then I saw, her face in recollection,
in disappointment. . . .

The candle between us flickered, was extinguished by its own wax.
I reached across the table to calm her. But she was calm and I strained

out of my chair, watching her mouth open, making its words—
a flower, one of those that climb on trellises, hidden in ivy; not

at graves but in gardens, grown by people who wake just to see
them opened. The mouths of children before speech. The eyes

of birds whose songs remove us from sleep. The dancer died and rose
to finish her dance. She told me this over dinner. I was rendered

speechless, as if in the Service, her wake before her burial. Her folded hands
across her breast. Her head at peace, framed inside its wooden box.

"He lost his hold and fell, taking me with him" *1909*

The canoe capsized because you misjudged the depth—thought it would be
a good place to stand and fish. We stood waist-deep in the channel,
the inverted craft like an unshucked cob floating between us.

We had followed the fury of terns spiralling the sky, diving for invisible
things all around us. We were looking for fish for you to catch. For you to
hook, reel in at the end of your line, hold in your wetted hands.

I imagine the sailor's hands were wet that made him lose his grip.
Another man (a pirate?) clings to his leg, together they hang from a rope
over a rough ocean rife with sharks. Our fall was nothing compared

to what theirs would be. *He lost his hold and fell, taking me with him.*
The title means: they fall—a misshapen fruit, conjoined wholes, will fall first
from the bough. Because of its weight. Because the painter knows

this, he paints them hanging, one from the other like dragonflies mating
in midair, flying by me as I cross the bridge over the bay.
People come to this bridge from other towns to drop baited hooks

into the channel. We must have looked strange from where they fish:
Two men paddling. Two men standing waist-deep in water.
In the painting the men are struggling against their fall, they still have

hope. You had hoped we would have luck that evening, hoped the trip
would rid me of my poor impression of fishing. I had hoped the terns were
wrong—knowing how a fish looks dying in air, its confused mouth

working like the mouth of a hungry bird. Birds mate in midflight, too,
meet suspended for a moment to make their young. The men fall, having
hung on until *his hold* was *lost*. The painter gives the impression

they might save themselves. But the title says otherwise. So the hope
one could harbor for them is short lived. Like a fish pulled from the
waves. Its mouth seems to breathe. It appears to be breathing not dying.

You were testing the depths with the canoe paddle to see if you could
stand. I didn't see what was coming until I was waist-deep in the water.
Our fall was nothing compared to what the sailors' endured. Which ever

sailor survived, who ever the speaker is—his account told by hindsight.
The account so deftly seen from a bird's-eye view, painted with a grace
suggesting the artist's voice, speaking of the place in which we all

hang suspended.

AT THE SYMPHONY

I envy the cellist with the sculpted barrel
between her knees.
I envy the violinist, the trainer of a mahogany bird
perched on his shoulder.
I admire them, I appreciate
each finger pulling and plucking, beckoning
silence into symphony.

The man on my left has fallen asleep,
his head bobs at my shoulder.
The old couple in front sink into their chairs,
a woman looks for someone behind her
through the small eye of her compact.
I am here in my uncoiling sweater, hair wet
from the rain. From my seat the musicians' faces
are hidden, their arms flail like branches
in a storm.

During intermission, I climb stairs
to the balcony. The statues, tucked into
niches peer out from their holes,
marble birds. They look across the hall at one another
with perfect, round eyes. I envy their smooth limbs,
their tilting grace, their ears. I envy
their supreme composure—
like the fish in my childhood tank,

who never knew I was there
as I tapped their glass walls,
straining to hear the sounds
from their singing, silent mouths.

MUSIC LESSONS

In the church, his hands over my eyes, the score
turned upside-down, I'd strain to gather the measures.
The notes, like swarms of bees I would pluck
from the air, replacing each in its comb,
my fingers thin and careful, piecing together the hive.

In the cup of his hands it smelled like soil.
I saw through his fingers, past the map of whorls,
as if my eyes were faceted: a child's drawing of a sheep,
a flag, the hallway, a hanging lamp, the double doors
leading out into the Pilgrim graveyard.

Every Friday, I followed the path through fields
and yards and roads, up the back stairs to the auditorium
where my coat would be laid on the radiator.
He would put my hands in mittens, his scarf trailing
like an empty leash. When I played well, he gave me

one perfect cherry tomato, saved from his garden. This I kept
unchewed, rattling in the trough beneath my teeth
and tongue. At home I played when the house was empty;
performing in the dark for the furniture, the wide mouth
of the fireplace, the windows with their swirling glass, letting in

evening, showing through its painted grid: a willow,
a garden, the car turning into the driveway, headlights
sweeping around the room. Each time I would jump from the bench,
run through the darkened rooms to the front door, my fingers
like a child's, cold and fumbling with the lock.

WORK

A tooth has five sides. The hygienist told me this
as she flossed the sides untouched by the brush.

A knife has five sides, she said, and you can clean
all five with a single wipe. This is not the case with the tooth.

Like a piece of paper? I asked. That's six, she said,
though I thought paper had just two sides.

My art teacher explained that good paper
has tooth. It accepts the ink from the etching plate best.

The etching plate—which is *bitten*—in its acid bath.
The paper with the best tooth must soak in water

to be damp when laid on the wiped plate
and both are pressed together: bitten plate,

biting paper and the ink passed between them.
I've pulled prints: it's like prying open the mouth

of a trap. And tacked the print on the wall
only to see an ink smear or nick or swipe, or my own finger's

print ruining the margin. Like the blood
from my mouth on the hygienist's blouse.

On the labcoat over her blouse—a corsage
I put there, or she uprooted from my mouth and placed

upon her breast. I was embarrassed. She looked down
and asked through her paper mask if I was all right:

The more you floss, the less bleeding there will be, she said.
Too much tooth and you lose the details, my teacher said,

relentless because he loved these things,
always covered with ink.

IN THE MUSEUM

I find the painting of Joan abandoning her
yarn. She parts the leaves of a low branch, her back to saints
snagged like laundry in the trees. The branch is a door
she opens or a curtain she divides.

I went to the high fields
flanked by woods, a slender path
like a flaw in the dense order of trees.
A pond in the clearing, its stench
a taste: cooked lily, stewed pollen, the rot
beneath the algae's shawl.

The arbor was silent except for its
grapes, heavy tongue-less bells.
The broad meadow's breast, a yellow bolt
unrolled, stitched with white boxes of hives.
In the bog the ground ballooned, broke
as breath will when held too long.

Her house has a clay-tiled roof, her window a leaded
pane. With eyes cast upward, she gazes beyond the frame—
beyond me standing outside it—away from her chore
and overturned chair, farther into the shadows

of unrendered trees.

JOHN SINGER SARGENT MURALS, BOSTON PUBLIC LIBRARY

How do these things happen? The murals are coated in soot. The saints
are vague, dimmed as if seen through a veil of smoke, which was the cause—
candles. Wax burned to the finest silt, light as air—like a breath, infected.

So. Neglect, lack of foresight—and light—combined to create a constant
evening for the saints to suffer in—making their stories even sadder
through further obscurity.

On either side of the marble staircase that leads to the murals sit two stone
    lions—
huge, rough hewn, guarding the library's foyer where a table is set up,
with pamphlets. *The advent of electricity*, states an informational card, *revealed—*

suddenly—how serious the damage was. Who knows when a shadow takes hold?
Either here or where our uncle was who lived so far away—farther—since he
    hadn't
spoken to us in years. The murals were so high up no one could see how
    ruined they were

and he, way up north, ignored us, let everything worsen—all of us in ignorance.
The card continues: *In an effort to show the need for restoration, experts have
    cleaned
a square foot of soot from the face of a male saint*. I forget which one, but I
    remember
the aperture of pure mural—his eyes emerging like the window-cut cloth,

surgical blue with its sterile view of skin, the unsuccessful slice and its neat

diagonal stitches. . . . The murals are ruined but will be repaired. Our uncle
harbored

his disease for years, and he died. There was no useful intervention, then or
now. . . .

The figures are shrouded and will remain so, even after restoration—

they will be coated despite their cleaning. Just as our uncle will be, though we
know

he was finally cleansed of what ruined him. The lions will remain, rough hewn,

obvious. I understand now. Like the saints, we have our stories. They have

their lessons, poised in their dim residue, eager, officious, privileged to recount

the difference: what it was to be consumed. How it is to be freed.

ON SEEING *FOX HUNT* BY WINSLOW HOMER, AFTER MANY YEARS

Crows chase a fox through deep snow, *tiring it to the point*
of exhaustion and death—so says the caption that accompanies
the painting. When I was young and saw the piece, I thought
the animals were playing—the fox cavorting with its outstretched
paw, the birds flapping comically above him like something out of

Aesop. Not quite. But despite my ignorance, the image remains true—
the crows are black, the fox is flame colored, the few berries dangling
from a stem, are red—red the way the snow will be, awash in the fox's
blood, after he has given up and is torn apart in the frozen moat
he has been driven to dig, *a doomed animal.* . . . Luckily, we are spared

this sight. The only violence in the frame is in the background
where a wave explodes: green foam against dark rocks. I hadn't
remembered the scene was set at seaside, but I see now the ocean
adds its own interpretation to the events, expressing in the breaking
wave—forever shattering, healing—a sacrifice beyond our

comprehension. It takes youth to witness such desperation and read it
as joy, raised as we are on the stories where beasts can speak and
reason—which they can, I'm still sure of it . . . but since those days
the crows have grown ravenous; the fox, leaping uselessly, knows
what is to come, and turns his face away from us.

FOUR

OPEN LETTER RE: THE GOOD FIGHT

The couple that lives above me doesn't sleep. We keep
the same hours. We always have. We, meaning you, me,

and now this couple. Although, you recently said you have
started to come home and go straight to bed. Fourteen hours

the other night. It can't be good. You said that. And when
you get up, you can't wait to get home and go back to bed.

On the train I imagine being held at gunpoint, not resisting.
You can relate. We've talked about this. *Do me the favor.*

We hate this conversation. But we have it. Which is odd.
That we say these things. These troubles. I always mean

to sound comforting when I say: *you can't shock me.*
Fourteen hours, though.

I admit I'm worried. For both of us. Being so *kindred.*
I don't even know the couple's names. We keep the same

hours. We, meaning the couple, me, and four or five
lighted windows across the street. I rarely turn on lights

in my room. Go about in the dark. Have I mentioned this?
Perhaps you do, too. But I can't imagine. We *are* separate.

Dear reader, you will not receive this, directly. Maybe. More on that later. You've probably been asleep for hours by now.

Maybe you're up? In the morning there's less time to think. The elevator, going down, carrying strangers. The train.

AN ATTEMPT

It was a rare moment in the city—where we are meant to be strong. Fear gave way to awe. I was in the Cathedral's garden. The ivy split, released a peacock. The blue caught my eye; all its eyes caught my eye—all its eyes, splayed out along the tail, which it dragged across the grass, a heavy net.

The children dragged bluefish alongside the boat having lured them with flies. The fish flew as they were yanked from the waves, like sparks jumping and spoons spinning in a sink's cloudy pool. I thought of the fish

while looking at the bird, a living jewel sullied in the garden shadows. I thought of you. Your gift to me a capacity for sympathy, mostly because at times I feel sorry for you. Not in the way I feel for the fish. Or the

bird whose beauty seemed absurd the longer I watched it. I'd detected nothing from the fish—meaning, I couldn't gauge if they felt the pain of their predicament. The bird was imperious toward me, so I limited my

empathy. But things have not been easy for you; I don't mean to say it's about beauty—because I ended up feeling pity for the bird, for it's useless spectrum of blues, odd little crown. As for the fish, their beauty is secret,

explicit only at certain angles. It's not really their silver that makes them worthwhile—meaning, it's not why they get hooked. But, again this is not about appearance—that's just a sad factor in the sum of your troubles.

Your blues. The bird cried a shrill childish cry—not like the children in
the boat who'd scored their catch. They were joyful. This was frightening,
worse than what I'd gotten used to in the city. And having learned to

determine balance in everything, I appraised the bird's voice to be
the ugliest thing about it. This practice is successful in the alienation of
imperfect things. Or things whose perfection is dismaying. Though, as I

said before, you gave me, or taught me—an odd distinction to make . . .
in me you vested an awareness of your pain. An exclusive pain, outside
the perimeter I'd drawn up for what I'd known. Is this what is meant by

education? Do we just believe the fish want to feed? Do we esteem
the slender-necked bird and never ask: what good are you? In the shadow
of the Cathedral, I found myself afraid, even though the day was
flawless. I saw the bird. You came to mind. I was afraid for you.

VOCATIONS

All the hanging plants spun
when I overwatered them. I remember the nest
that came down, shredded, as I sprayed the rafters.
I remember it

now, as I stand in the church.
The vaults arc like stems or teeth
of a comb, bent along a finger. Candles
are snuffed by children lost in swinging robes.

I do not understand the windows with their chiseled
light. The incense steams
and winds into my sweater. I come here to stare
as the bells toss away

their chimes. I go out the bronze doors
into the rain-beaten day. I go home,
obscured in the elevator's
tiny mirror: gaunt and drenched.

Water has come in under the sill.
I strip off the wet clothes and leave them
where they drop. A man in the street
clears leaves from the sewer with his hands.

EVERY HOUR HERE

Someone else is up, ringing the cathedral bells, paying out the tolls
into a dawn that disintegrates like a newspaper losing its words
in a ring of rainwater. Here the chimes are loud, launched into air

like a trumpet's blast. In Greece, lying in my narrow bed I heard
church bells, a voice more bird than chime, reaching my ear having
fled from its mouth through the dense olive groves. All bells have

mouths. Heads and crowns, too. The head of the girl I saw from
the diner's window was crowned with ringlets. As when plastic ribbon
is frayed, made to curl. Or the shape a finger makes spiraling in the air

before landing on a spot in the atlas: where to go next. Here the bells go
all night. Someone must live in the tower, sleep beneath the ropes.
I lie awake, ten stories above the street of changing leaves.

At first light two men resume drilling into the bricks across
the way. They stand on a metal cart that hangs by a single hook, at night
the cart swings in the winds that come off the river. The paper reports

needless deaths because of things like this. Because repairs
are done poorly. In Greece I passed by a crew fixing a well,
an ancient well, said to grant wisdom, maybe eternal life. Its taste

was tart, metallic, like snow off a car's hood or a hot spoon
drawn from its honeyed cup. The water was not worth what it promised
because it was hard to swallow. Though I drank it the day I walked up

the mountain toward the monasteries where old monks gardened,
white-washed around their doors. The work across the street has my
neighbors craning out their windows. The racket draws them out

like birds from birdhouse holes. For hours the men in the cart
drill into the bricks—the pattern is ruined as the problem is revealed.
For years the cathedral has been under repair. Under nets and scaffolding.

Through this heavy veil the bells' sound escapes—fish the net cannot trap.
Boats dumped their fish in a silver heap for old Greek women
to buy. Coins fished from their purses, dropped from hand to hand

or into the box for funds to build a children's theater underneath
the apse. The cathedral cellar is a maze of rooms: a school, a concert hall.
In Greece, I peered under the altar of an ancient church and saw

its flooded crypt, fish circling lichen-covered columns, their slim shadows
staining the floor's mosaic. The water corroded the church because
of salt. Because of thirst I drank the water from the broken

well, it had a yellow tint, tasted like a coin in the mouth—but renowned
to grant wisdom, even immortality. At what price? The tolls spill
from the tower. I bought a ticket, climbed the flights to inspect them:

green, massive and cold, with winged figures embossed on their sides.
On their *waists*. The bell's parts have the same names as body parts.
Ten stories above the tree-lined street I see the leaves spiraling.

How did these red leaves rise to spin their aimless paths outside my
window? In Greece the chimes came to me in bed, entered as the angel
whose work it is to repossess. I am convinced: had I not drunk, despite

the taste, despite the myth . . . where would I be? Here the leaves are
red as the girl's crown of hair, pouring from her head like a fountain's steady
spill. And the newspapers report falling bricks, people struck

dead as they pass below. Here the cathedral is ruined, rebuilt with all
the wrong blocks. And uniformed school children pour out its doors, run
with drawings that flutter at their sides like wings, thin paper wings.

ON 9TH STREET

one block from the plaque showing where Marianne Moore
once lived, a woman on the sidewalk spray-paints her bicycle
white. She has removed the tires, gears and pedals, put down
newspaper over the pavement to protect it.

Without its parts the bicycle looks strange, unwieldy
as she struggles to apply an even coat—struggles in the way
the farmhand would, wrestling with our sheep, flipping and pinning
them in the paddock as I gathered the oily wool that fell from the shears.

Gradually, the bicycle glows white against the evening, seeping
through the canopy of new leaves. I noticed it when I crossed
the street: it looked like a swan, a snake, it was the terrible shape
of my grade school gym teacher, outlined in crude strokes on the road—

from the window of the bus we could look down on her,
geometric, the inhuman angles she had assumed after being hit
and thrown. She used to play a tape, make us square-dance around
a striped parachute, insist we promenade in pairs, arms

linked the way the ankles must be crossed—locked to secure
the ewe, the ram, to shave its neck and breast where the wool is softest.
Soon the bicycle is complete, white, without blemish or visible under-
paint. The woman admires her work, balances the bike with one hand

on the spattered papers. What would that poet say, I wonder, all such proximity? *Some kinds of gratitude are trying?* I think of my teacher, her shape disappearing into the pavement with every rainstorm. *We should like to know how that was done.*

ORNITHOLOGY

They looked like dogs out in the water—that size—
only they were loons in their winter plumage;
white on their wings and heads; I could find them

instantly when they surfaced, suddenly
in water that had not been broken.
The sky was the color of a bleached tarp,

the same sky in the city when weather
threatens, troubles the plastic bag in the tree—not
a bird—a bag has been snared in the tree. It calls

above my head. I called to the far-off boat because
I was alone on the beach.
On the boardwalk, loud gulls around a woman throwing

scraps of bread. The noise was harsh, they fought
the food out of her hand. Not the same woman who feeds
birds in the park near the bus stop—her flock

is still. This woman looks as if she's sowing a field, the birds
around her like the blocks of stones laid out
for the cathedral's repair—the facade is always losing

its saints. One by one they return, scrubbed clean,
newly painted, displayed like dolls over the bronze doors.
Across the street in the community garden small birds bathe

in dirt. When I passed by the overgrown lot, I thought
they were mice burrowing for shelter. I had forgotten
I'd seen birds do this before. They fluttered in the dust like

sufferers, separated by a fence, a screen along the ground
because rats get in, eat the plants. At first I thought the birds were
vermin since it is a problem in this neighborhood. Even their

sounds led me to believe it, a song along the lines of a scream.
But I was stupid to think this, because at once their convoy lifted
and I was surrounded, all around me they exploded, opened and closed

like books.

EDIBLE FLOWERS

The idea was that the garden would give us something back—our hopes
strung along the humblest vine like the flowers retreating from their raised bed

infested with slugs. The idea was that the slugs would die in the tins of beer
we set over the soil—gray bodies (are they called bodies when they're this

shape?) floating in flat gold liquid. That didn't work—everything was eaten.
Except the flowers, which crawled across the grass, up the fence to safety. They

are full of life—and color—yet taste like nothing. Not even like the greens
they're served with; their petals are waxy, only their organs have the bitter

gristle of tears—the tears fallen to the grass by our family plot. Once, my brother
described a many-flamed torch, aimed at the ground and burning it. It was in

winter, in a cemetery—I think it was in Providence. In order to accommodate
the casket, he explained, the ground had to be thawed. No one in my family

approves of burial, even though our plots await us—slender strips of perfect
grass, like the one our uncle inhabits, locked inside a red antique box. These

garden flowers are reddish orange with white stems. At dinner, they look like
specks of fire, competing with the candles. At sunset, the radio reports

a frost is expected. Remember, we're told, to cover your gardens—we won't, so
the slugs will freeze on the leaves they consume. The dog, kept out by the fence,

will eat everything else: bark, bulbs, pocked yellow apples. The crows eat
blueberries in the meadow. I thought this was strange, since I usually see them

eating what's dead on the road. . . . Anyhow, last night I found four deer eating
from the bird feeder. I watched them until they saw me and ran away, their

white tails flickering like the whitecaps in the harbor where the salty air drifts
up through the meadow into the garden where I inspect the tins, always

empty. At dusk, the flowers look withered, but they are only asleep,
their colors safely enclosed, arousing in me an odd sense of envy. Asked about it

now, my brother is unclear as to what he saw that night—blue flames hissing,
spraying up snow and mist . . . that is how I see it. The memory is now mine

in the same way the garden has been taken over, along with everything else
that is edible. When I die, I want the ocean to ingest me. Each member of my

family wants the same thing only in different parts of the world, which is
interesting—that we've talked about it at all, and because, all bodies of water

are connected underground. Our wish is to be united when it's all over.
But for now, our wish is to reap some simple reward—more than a handful

of split tomatoes and three flimsy leeks. You can't make a meal of that.
What can I do in the face of such disappointment but pull off the unappetizing

blooms and place them on my tongue—tasteless but invaluable
like a coin in the mouth of the dead.

LIBERTY ISLAND

On the street the trees throw off their whiteness, petals
like the paper discs a hole punch makes or confetti
poured over the head of the girl who gave the party
where we met.

It was winter, downtown the snow was dyed pink where
a red envelope had been dropped, forgotten. All the parked cars
were trapped in snowbanks.

We sat with our drinks by the window, a swag of postcards clipped
to a string on the wall. You told me about the island, the remote house
where, to see the ocean over the trees, you would stand
on the pitched roof, hugging the crumbling chimney.

Outside, on the sidewalk, all the freezing people grimaced,
waiting for us to give up our table.

And then what? At the concert we watched pairs of players,
perfectly aligned, attuned, making their beautiful noise out of the air
we coughed and whispered into. And then? This morning

what is saved? The daylight. I wake to the steady song of a bird; no,
a truck backing up in the street.

In the park with its view of Liberty Island I sit by the freshly planted
bed, the bulb's results lolling—fluted flowers in a neat line
pale yellow and white. Everyone stops to watch them nod

in the new spring air. Today the trees are dressed, filled with fronds,
the water is glass all around us.

WHY SPEAK?

Don't you see? There's nothing to be said, no need to say a thing
when our hands meet during the reading and our fifth fingers link,
hinge, hang locked for a moment so we both lose our
focus on the poor reader emoting from the podium.

Let our lips be the shut clasp of a coin purse, my sister's:
red leather, gold clasp like two fingers about to snap. That
was the first test, the doctor snapped his fingers beside my sister's ear.
Eventually, he shaved the side of her head, removed her misshapen

drum. They thought she was deaf. And she was. She spent all her time
with animals. Once I saw a bird eat seed from her hand. From her mitten.
It stayed there to pick out the seeds buried in the knit.
Not like the boy I watched for hours in an Italian town square—

he wore scraps of bread like badges and pigeons ate off his body. He stood
still, as a statue, and the flock stained him with their paste. My sister
was more like a perch, a feeder, no more than a table set with its cloth
and plate—but alive in the way flowers in a bowl are alive, even though they

have been cut, set in the center to die among diners. She didn't die, she got
her hearing back, the drum removed or repaired, the drum—*the skin* a friend
of mine would say, referring specifically to the part that's struck with a stick.
Don't you see? She couldn't hear a thing except what she thought

the animals were saying. Silence in the barn. Quiet in the paddock. What
was there to hear? All the reader wants, breathless at the podium is to give

his words. Amazing, that sound, his rifling through the pages. Sheet over
sheet, my dropped music, late to my lesson, littering the stairwell

of the music school. After the two hours were up my teacher would lock
the building while I waited on the steps for my ride. You see, we had
nothing to say outside that room where our pianos stood like black bulls
waiting to charge. Mute, I played for him. Miming, he

criticized me, waving what meant *Largo!* Always Largo. Because I played
too fast. He beat his palm on the bench. Snapped his fingers at my ear so I
would hear exactly how it was written. The reader wants nothing more
than to move us by what he has written. I wrote my teacher to tell him

I was ending my lessons. I suspected that he was dying. And he was.
In his sickness he instructed me with silence. Years later, a woman in my Italian
class told me she'd known him, told me he died in the house where he'd once
invited me, where we played Christmas duets for his guests.

She said he died in June, attacked in his garden. His heart attacked while he
was working in the garden. I was struck by the news, for I had not
been able to forget him. Though I had left him as one leaves flowers
at the grave of the deceased. In memoriam. Except he hadn't died yet.

When I ended my lessons he was alive, silent but brimming with sound—
what the unstruck drum suggests by its wide, stretched skin. I imagine him
stretched out in his garden. Calling out. Calling out for someone to come
and help. There was nothing I could do. Don't you see? I had quit playing

in favor of . . . there is nothing I can say to explain this. My sister received her hearing from the surgeon's hand. I left my lessons because they haunted my head. She lay in her hospital bed encircled by flowers, her slow speech, strange, like a voice speaking underwater. Underground.

Did they bury him in the garden? I had seen it that winter on my visit to play for the strangers. The garden was silenced by snow, the arbor shrouded, the dead vines frozen, locked around their posts—not like our fingers, clasping for a moment while the reader sang his work. . . .

Because vines live this way: climb, die, climb, die. Like flowers: bloom, wither . . . or birds: soar, shot from the sky. Don't you see? Who knows what to make of that moment? Our hands . . . we don't plan these things. We don't need the meaning. So why speak about it? Why speak?

Notes

[p. 43] *"So the treasure was divided" 1905,* includes lines in italics from Thomas Hardy's "During Wind and Rain," (*Selected Poems of Thomas Hardy,* Collier Books, 1966).

[p. 48] *"Her head and shoulders hung over the space without" 1904,* includes lines in italics from William Wordsworth's "Elegiac Stanzas," (*The Norton Anthology of Poetry,* Fourth Edition, W. W. Norton & Company, 1996).

[p. 73] "On 9th Street," contains lines in italics from two Marianne Moore poems: "Voracities and Verities Sometimes are Interacting" and "The Icosasphere," (*Marianne Moore: Complete Poems,* Penguin Books, 1994).